Book Cover by Tukotuku Publishing

Illustrations by Tukotuku Publishing

First edition 2025

Print ISBN: 978-1-991366-23-8

Ebook ISBN: 978-1-991366-24-5

MICHELLE HUIRAMA

TUKOTUKU PUBLISHING

A Hug in My Heart

Helping Young Hearts Heal After Losing A Grandmother

Michelle Huirama

For you, sweet heart.

If you are missing your Grandmother, this book is for you.

May it remind you that it's okay to feel sad,

to smile at memories,

and to love someone forever

even when they're no longer here.

Your Grandmother's love is still with you,

tucked safely in your heart, like a hug that never fades.

Contents

Hi there,   1

Understanding Grief   3
Chapter 1

Reflection 1   8
What is Grief?

Reflection 2   10

Reflection 3   12
Why Do We Feel Sad?

Reflection 4   14
Happy Memories

Reflection 5   16
Everyone Grieves Differently

Reflection 6   18
A Message

Reflection 7   20
How do you feel today?

Memories of Grandma   23
Chapter 2

Reflection 1   27
Sharing Happy Moments

Reflection 2   29
Sharing a Memory

Reflection 3   31
Creating a Memory Book

Reflection 4   34
Decorating your Book

Reflection 5   36
Writing Letters to Grandma

Reflection 6   39
How are you feeling today?

Emotions Are Important   42
Chapter 3

Reflection 1   48
Identifying Your Feelings

Reflection 2   51
Drawing Shapes

Reflection 3   53
Expressing Anger and Sadness

Reflection 4   57
Drawing Feelings

Reflection 5   60
Finding Joy in Memories

Reflection 6   62
Draw the Memory

Creative Expression Through Art   64
Chapter 4

Reflection 1   68
Through Art Drawing Your Feelings

Reflection 2   70

Reflection 3   72

Reflection 4   74

Reflection 5   76
Moment Reflection

Reflection 6   78
Paint It

Reflection 7   80
Crafting a Tribute

Reflection 8   82
What Did you Make?

Reflection 9   84

Reflection 10   86

Reflection 11   88

Reflection 12   90

Sharing Stories from the Heart   92
Chapter 5 - Encourages reflection, creativity, and emotional expressions

Reflection 1   96

Reflection 2   98

Reflection 3   101

Reflection 4   104

Reflection 5   106

Reflection 6   109

Reflection 7   111

Journaling for Kids   113
Chapter 6

Reflection 1   117

Reflection 2   119

Reflection 3   121

Reflection 4   123

Reflection 5   125

Reflection 6   127

Reflection 7   129

Reflection 8   131

Reflection 9   133

Reflection 10   135

Comfort in Community   137
Chapter 7

Reflection 1   141

Reflection 2   142

Reflection 3   145

Reflection 4   147

Reflection 5   149

Finding Calm Inside   151
Chapter 8

Reflection 1   156
Try a Breathing Exercise

Reflection 2   158
Create a Memory Drawing

Reflection 3   160
What's in My Calm Space?

Reflection 4   162
Mindful Moment Journal Prompt

Reflection 5   164
My Comfort Plan

Honoring Nana Through Memories   166
Chapter 9

Reflection 1   171
My Memory Tree Plan

Reflection 2   173
My Memory Box Ideas

Reflection 3   175
Create and Celebrate

Reflection 4   177
A Letter to My Granny

Reflection 5   179
My Special Day Plan

Learning About Feelings   181
Chapter 10

Reflection 1   185
Color My Feeling

Reflection 2   187
What I Want to Say

Reflection 3   189
Book Connection

Reflection 4   191
Talking Practice

Reflection 5   193
Act It Out

Grief Games and Gentle Sharing   196
Chapter 11

Reflection 1   201
Draw a Memory Game

Reflection 2   203
Feelings Charades

Reflection 3   205
Movie Reflection

Reflection 4   207
Journal Starter

Reflection 5   209
Nature Icebreaker

Nature and Healing   211
Chapter 12

Reflection 1   216
Create Your Memory Garden

Reflection 2   218
Nature Walk Reflection

Reflection 3   220
Nature Scavenger Hunt

Reflection 4   222
My Nature Journal Prompt

Talking and Listening Together   224
Chapter 13

Reflection 1   230
My Talking Place

Reflection 2   232
Memory Art

Reflection 3   234
Story Connection

Reflection 4   236
Listen With Your Heart

Reflection 5   238
Safe Space Checklist

A Hug That Stays in Our Hearts   240
Chapter 14

Final Reflections   243

Gentle Reminders for Grownups   250
Supporting Grieving Children

Let's Meet Michelle Huirama   253

With Love   255

A Healing Grief Series   257
for children aged 7 and up

Hi there,

If you're holding this book in your hands, it might be because someone very special to you—like your Grandmother—has passed away. And if that's true, I want to start by saying something really important: **I'm so sorry.** Losing someone you love hurts in a way that words can't always explain.

This book was made just for you. It's here to help you understand what grief is, why you feel the way you do, and how to keep going even when your heart feels heavy. Inside these pages, you'll find kind words, gentle ideas, and comforting thoughts to help you feel a little less alone.

You don't have to be strong all the time. You don't have to "move on" or forget. Your love for your Grandmother is still with you—and always will be. She lives in your memories, your stories, your laugh, and the hug you'll always carry in your heart.

Let's take this journey together—one page, one feeling, one hug at a time.

With love,
Someone who cares

Understanding Grief

Chapter 1

In this chapter, we'll explore what grief really means and how it feels inside our hearts. When someone as special as Nana dies, it can feel like everything changes, and it can be hard to understand what is happening in your heart and mind. You might feel lots of feelings all at once—sad, angry, lonely, or even a little numb. That's what grief is: a mix of feelings that come from missing someone you love so much.

We'll talk about why you feel sad, how grief can look different for each person, and ways to share what's going on inside of you. You'll learn that it's perfectly okay to have these big feelings, and you don't have to hide them. Grief can be like a storm that comes and goes, and together we'll find ways to remember Grandma's love, even on hard days.

So take a deep breath, be gentle with yourself, and know that you are not alone on this journey. Let's discover how to hold on to your memories, while giving your heart a safe place to feel, heal, and remember.

What Is Grief?

Grief is what you feel when someone you love is no longer with you. It can feel like a storm of emotions—sadness, confusion, anger, or even emptiness—all swirling around inside. If you've lost your Granny, you might feel like there's a hole in your heart that no one else can see. That feeling? That's grief.

You might find yourself crying one minute and laughing at a memory the next. Some days you might not want to talk to anyone. Other days, you might want to talk about her nonstop. This is all part of grieving. It doesn't follow a straight line, and everyone goes through it in their own way—and in their own time.

One thing that can help is remembering all the love you shared. Think about the stories she told, the sound of her laugh, her hugs, her smell, or the way she always knew just what to say. These memories are like little stars that can light up your heart when it feels dark.

You don't have to hide how you feel. Your emotions matter, and it's okay to let them out.

Why Do You Feel Sad?

Sadness comes when someone we love is no longer here to talk to, hug, or laugh with. That sadness shows just how deeply you loved—and were loved. It's a reflection of the bond you had with your Nonna.

You might feel like crying. You might feel like doing nothing. You might even feel mad that she's gone. These feelings are normal. Don't try to push them away or pretend you're okay if you're not.

Talking can really help. Tell someone you trust how you're feeling. They might have felt the same way when they lost someone too. You can also talk out loud to your Nan if it helps. Just because she's not physically here doesn't mean the love disappears.

Sadness won't last forever. It changes over time. And sometimes, you'll notice moments of peace slipping in between the tears—especially when you remember something she used to say or do that made you laugh.

Everyone Grieves Differently

Your grief is yours—and it won't look like anyone else's. You might notice your siblings, cousins, or friends dealing with loss in different ways. Some might talk about it all the time. Others might stay quiet. That's okay.

You don't have to feel the same way every day, and you don't have to heal at the same pace as someone else. Some kids find comfort in being around people. Others might need time alone. Trust what feels right for you.

You can also express your grief in your own way. Maybe you like to draw, write stories, or just sit and think. However you choose to remember your Gran and process your feelings—that's valid.

There's no "right" way to grieve. What matters most is being kind to yourself as you figure it all out.

Reflection 1

What is Grief?

This reflection is to help you explore your feelings after losing someone special like your Grandma, You can write or draw your answers. There are no wrong answers—this is just for you.

1. What does grief feel like to you?

Todays Date:

My Feelings Today

Circle how you're feeling right now (you can choose more than one):

Happy   Sad   Angry   Confused   Calm
Missing Grandma   Loved

Then write or draw about your feelings below

Reflection 2

2. What are some things you remember doing with your Nonna?

You can write or draw your answers

Todays Date:

My Feelings Today

Circle how you're feeling right now (you can choose more than one):

Happy   Sad   Angry   Confused   Calm
Missing Nonna   Loved

Then write or draw about your feelings below

Reflection 3

Why Do We Feel Sad?

3. What makes you feel the saddest when you think about your Gran?

You can write or draw your answers

Todays Date:

My Feelings Today

Circle how you're feeling right now (you can choose more than one):

Happy   Sad   Angry   Confused   Calm
Missing Gran   Loved

Then write or draw about your feelings below

Reflection 4

Happy Memories

4. What's one memory that makes you smile when you think about her?

You can write or draw your answers

Todays Date:

My Feelings Today

Circle how you're feeling right now (you can choose more than one):

Happy   Sad   Angry   Confused   Calm
Missing Granma   Loved

Then write or draw about your feelings below

Reflection 5

Everyone Grieves Differently

5. How do you like to share your feelings? (Talking, drawing, writing, etc.)

You can write or draw your answers

Todays Date:

My Feelings Today

Circle how you're feeling right now (you can choose more than one):

Happy   Sad   Angry   Confused   Calm
Missing Granny   Loved

Then write or draw about your feelings below

Reflection 6

A Message

6. If you could write a message to your Nan, what would you say?

You can write or draw your answers

Todays Date:

My Feelings Today

Circle how you're feeling right now (you can choose more than one):

Happy   Sad   Angry   Confused   Calm
Missing Nan   Loved

Then write or draw about your feelings below

Reflection 7

How do you feel today?

How are you feeling today?

Circle the feelings you've had since your Nonna passed away: You can also write about that feeling

Sad

Angry

Confused

Grateful

Lonely

Loved

Hopeful

You can draw your own emoji or write another feeling:

Memories of Grandma

Chapter 2

In this chapter, we'll explore how remembering the good times with your Grandma can help your heart feel a little lighter. Even though she isn't here the same way anymore, the memories you shared together can still bring comfort, smiles, and even giggles. It's okay to feel sad and happy at the same time — that's part of how love keeps shining through.

You'll learn fun and meaningful ways to celebrate those moments, like making a memory book or writing letters to your Nana. These activities can help you hold on to the stories, laughter, and hugs you still treasure. Whenever you miss her, you can return to these memories, like cozy blankets wrapping around your heart.

Let's discover together how talking about happy times can remind you of Gran's love, and help you carry it forward with you every day.

Sharing Happy Moments

Thinking about your Nonna might bring up a lot of different feelings—sometimes you'll feel sad, but sometimes you might smile, too. That's the magic of memories. Remembering happy times, like baking cookies together, singing her favorite songs, or snuggling under a warm blanket for bedtime stories, helps keep her close—even when she's not here.

You can keep those memories alive by sharing them out loud. Tell a family member about the time your Granny made you laugh so hard your belly hurt. Or whisper your favorite memory to yourself when you miss her most. Each time you talk about her, it's like giving her a hug with your heart.

Creating a Memory Book

A memory book is a beautiful way to collect and keep all your special moments with your Nan in one place. You can fill it with drawings, photos, little notes, or even a list of her favorite sayings or things she used to do that made you feel safe and loved.

Make your book as bright or as cozy as you want—it's your space to remember. You could draw the garden you picked flowers in, write a poem about how her hugs felt, or include a recipe she taught you. There's no right or wrong way—just your way.

And if it feels right, share your memory book with someone else. Looking through it together can bring smiles, giggles, and sometimes even a few tears—these are all signs of love.

Writing Letters to your Gram

When your heart feels full of things you wish you could tell her, try writing a letter to your Oma. You can start with "Dear Grandma" and just let your thoughts flow. Tell her about your day, something that made you think of her, or something you miss. It's okay if you cry, and it's okay if you laugh too. She would want you to feel everything.

You might tuck your letter into your memory book, keep it under your pillow, or place it somewhere special. Some kids like to imagine their words floating up to her, carried by the wind or stars. However you do it, writing a letter is a way of saying, "I love you, and I'm still thinking about you."

Reflection 1

Sharing Happy Moments

1. Think about a time when you and Nana laughed together or did something special.

Draw or write about it below:

Todays Date:

My Feelings Today

Circle how you're feeling right now (you can choose more than one):

Happy   Sad   Angry   Confused   Calm
Missing Nana   Loved

Then write or draw about your feelings below

Reflection 2

Sharing a Memory

2. Can you tell someone about this memory today? Who would you like to share it with? Draw or write about it below:

Answer:

Todays Date:

My Feelings Today

Circle how you're feeling right now (you can choose more than one):

Happy   Sad   Angry   Confused   Calm
Missing Nonna   Loved

Then write or draw about your feelings below

Reflection 3

Creating a Memory Book

3. List or draw three things you'd like to include in your memory book about Grandma

1.

2.

3.

Todays Date:

My Feelings Today

Circle how you're feeling right now (you can choose more than one):

Happy   Sad   Angry   Confused   Calm
Missing Grandma   Loved

Then write or draw about your feelings below

Reflection 4

Decorating your Book

4. What colors or decorations will you use to make your book feel like Granma? Draw or write about it below:

Answer:

Todays Date:

My Feelings Today

Circle how you're feeling right now (you can choose more than one):

Happy   Sad   Angry   Confused   Calm
Missing Granma   Loved

Then write or draw about your feelings below

Reflection 5

Writing Letters to Grandma

5. Use the space below to start a letter to Grandma. Begin with 'Dear Grandma,' and write anything you'd like to tell her.

Dear Grandma,

Remember: There's no wrong way to remember someone you love. Your heart will always know the way.

Todays Date:

My Feelings Today

Circle how you're feeling right now (you can choose more than one):

Happy Sad Angry Confused Calm
Missing Grandma Loved

Then write or draw about your feelings below

Reflection 6

How are you feeling today?

Circle the feelings you've had today: You can also write about that feeling

Sad

Angry

Confused

Grateful

Lonely

Loved

Hopeful

You can draw your own emoji or write another feeling:

Emotions Are Important

Chapter 3

In this chapter, we'll gently explore all the different feelings you might have after losing your Granny. Grief can feel big and confusing, with many emotions swirling around your heart. Sometimes you might feel sad, angry, scared, or even a little bit okay — and that's all perfectly normal.

Together, we'll talk about how to name those feelings, share them, and express them in ways that feel safe. You'll discover how drawing, writing, talking, or even just sitting quietly can help your heart feel lighter.

It's okay to feel a lot of things all at once — it means you loved Gran very much. By learning how to understand your feelings, you'll see that they are a special part of keeping her memory alive, and a way for your heart to heal.

Identifying Your Feelings

When someone we love passes away—like your Granmama—it can stir up so many feelings inside. You might feel sad one moment, angry the next, and then maybe even a little confused. That's completely okay. Emotions are your heart's way of speaking when things are hard to explain.

Sometimes you might not have the words to say how you feel—and that's okay too. You can show your feelings through drawing, painting, writing, or even just sitting quietly and thinking. You could draw a memory of your Nan, or use colors to show what's going on inside. You might be surprised how much better you feel just by letting it out.

Books and stories about other kids who are grieving can also help. When you read about someone who has felt what you're feeling, it makes you feel less alone. And maybe you'll even feel a little bit stronger knowing others have found ways to keep going too.

Journaling is another gentle way to explore your heart. You can write about your favorite memories with your Oma, what you miss the most, or even what made you laugh together. Your journal becomes your safe place—a private world where you can be yourself and feel however you need to feel.

And always remember—feelings aren't wrong or bad. They're part of your healing journey. Letting them out, even in small ways, helps your heart feel lighter over time.

Expressing Anger and Sadness

Sometimes grief shows up as tears. Other times, it shows up as anger or frustration. You might feel mad that your Nonna is gone. You might feel it's unfair. That's all normal. Grief can be like a storm—loud, wild, and heavy—but even storms don't last forever.

One of the best things you can do is to do something with your feelings. Try splashing your feelings onto a page with colors, scribbles, or shapes. Or write a poem that shows how much you miss her. Art doesn't have to be pretty—it just has to be real. Your feelings are real, and they matter.

You don't have to go through it alone either. If you feel safe, talk to someone you trust—maybe a parent, a teacher, or a counselor. Telling someone how you feel can lift a bit of the sadness from your chest. You don't have to carry it all by yourself.

Sometimes, other kids feel the same way you do. In support groups, you might meet kids who also miss someone they love. You can cry together, share together, and slowly—heal together.

Remember: being sad or angry doesn't mean you're not doing okay. It just means you loved deeply. And that's something truly beautiful.

Identifying Your Feelings

In this chapter, we'll gently explore all the different feelings you might have after los-

MICHELLE HUIRAMA

ing your Nana. Grief can feel big and confusing, with many emotions swirling around your heart. Sometimes you might feel sad, angry, scared, or even a little bit okay — and that's all perfectly normal.

Together, we'll talk about how to name those feelings, share them, and express them in ways that feel safe. You'll discover how drawing, writing, talking, or even just sitting quietly can help your heart feel lighter.

It's okay to feel a lot of things all at once — it means you loved Nanny very much. By learning how to understand your feelings, you'll see that they are a special part of keeping her memory alive, and a way for your heart to heal.

Finding Joy in Memories

Even when someone we love is gone, the love doesn't disappear. It lives on in our memories—in the smell of a favorite cookie, the sound of a laugh, or the way the sunlight hits a certain chair. These little things can bring smiles through the tears.

You can honor those memories by creating something beautiful. Maybe you make a memory book or draw your happiest moment with your Grandmother. Maybe you write her a letter or tell her a joke you wish she could hear. These things don't make the sadness vanish, but they can remind you of the love that still surrounds you.

Journaling can help you hold onto joyful memories too. Write down your favorite things about your Grandma—her stories, her hugs, her laugh. These are treasures you can come back to when you're missing her most.

Sometimes, just being outside in the fresh air helps. Take a walk, sit under a tree, or watch the clouds drift by. Nature has a gentle way of helping us feel connected again—to ourselves and to those we miss.

Even though your Granny isn't here the way she used to be, she's still with you—in every memory, in every smile, in every heartbeat. That love never goes away.

Reflection 1

Identifying Your Feelings

1. What are three feelings you've had lately when thinking about your Nonna ? For example, maybe you felt happy or maybe you felt nothing,there is no right or wrong.

1.

2.

3.

Todays Date:

My Feelings Today

Circle how you're feeling right now (you can choose more than one):

Happy   Sad   Angry   Confused   Calm
Missing Nonna   Loved

Then write or draw about your feelings below

Reflection 2

Drawing Shapes

2. Color Your Feelings:

Draw a shape or use colors that match how you feel today. For example, blue might be a calm or sad day, red might feel angry or warm.

Todays Date:

My Feelings Today

Circle how you're feeling right now (you can choose more than one):

Happy   Sad   Angry   Confused   Calm
Missing Gran   Loved

Then write or draw about your feelings below

Reflection 3

Expressing Anger and Sadness

3. What helps you feel better when you're angry or sad?

• Talking to someone

- Drawing or painting

- Playing outside

• Listening to music

• Something else:

Todays Date:

My Feelings Today

Circle how you're feeling right now (you can choose more than one):

Happy   Sad   Angry   Confused   Calm
Missing Nan   Loved

Then write or draw about your feelings below

Reflection 4

Drawing Feelings

4. Write or draw one thing that made you feel really sad and one thing that helped a little:

Sad Thing:

Helpful Thing:

Todays Date:

My Feelings Today

Circle how you're feeling right now (you can choose more than one):

 Happy   Sad   Angry   Confused   Calm
Missing Granma   Loved

Then write or draw about your feelings below

Reflection 5

Finding Joy in Memories

5. What is one happy memory you have of your Granny? Draw or write about it below:

Todays Date:

My Feelings Today

Circle how you're feeling right now (you can choose more than one):

Happy   Sad   Angry   Confused   Calm
Missing Granny   Loved

Then write or draw about your feelings below

Reflection 6

Draw the Memory

6. Draw that happy memory in the space below:

Todays Date:

My Feelings Today

Circle how you're feeling right now (you can choose more than one):

Happy   Sad   Angry   Confused   Calm
Missing Gran   Loved

Then write or draw about your feelings below

Creative Expression Through Art

Chapter 4

In this chapter, we'll discover how art can help your heart heal. Sometimes it's hard to say how sad, confused, or lonely you feel after losing your Nana — but drawing can help you say it without words.

We'll talk about how to use colors, shapes, and even simple pictures to show what's happening inside you. You might draw a happy memory, a picture of Gran's smile, or even a rainbow to remind you of hope. You'll also find out how making crafts or painting can turn your love for Oma into something beautiful you can see and hold.

Remember: art doesn't have to be perfect. It just has to come from your heart.

Drawing Your Feelings

Sometimes, our hearts feel so full of emotion that it's hard to find the right words. That's where drawing comes in. Drawing can be like talking without speaking—it helps you show what you feel inside. If you're missing your Nan or feeling sad, pick up your pencils, crayons, or markers and just start. Maybe you'll draw a memory you shared, or maybe you'll draw how your heart feels today. Whatever you create, it's yours—and it's important.

You could even make a little memory sketchbook just for her. Page by page, you can fill it with drawings of her smile, her favorite things, or special moments you spent together. This kind of art isn't about being perfect—it's about being real. Your drawings can help you feel a little lighter and remind you of the love that's always with you.

Painting Memories

Painting is like adding color to your memories. You don't have to be an expert. You just have to feel. Maybe there's a sunset that reminds you of your Granny, or flowers that look like the ones she used to grow. Maybe you want to paint something that shows both your sadness and your love. It's okay to mix emotions on the canvas. Every brushstroke is a piece of your heart.

You might even paint while music plays or while you're sitting in the quiet. Let your feelings guide you. If you're not sure where to start, just begin with your favorite color and see what happens. Art doesn't always have to make sense—it just has to make you feel a little more understood.

Crafting a Tribute

You can also make something beautiful that helps you feel close to your Gram—something special that keeps her memory alive. This could be a memory box, a homemade card, or even a poem written on colored paper. Think about what reminds you of her. Was there a song she sang? A phrase she always said? A scent that makes you think of her hugs? Use these pieces to build your tribute.

Decorate your tribute however you like—glitter, stickers, ribbon, paint—whatever makes you smile. Keep it somewhere safe and special. And whenever you want, you can go back to it and remember how much she meant to you.

You could even invite family members to join you in creating something together. Sharing stories while you create can help everyone feel closer. Grief can be heavy, but when we create from the heart, we turn some of that heaviness into love we can see and hold.

Reflection 1

Through Art Drawing Your Feelings

1. Draw a picture of how you feel today. Use colors that match your emotions.

Todays Date:

My Feelings Today

Circle how you're feeling right now (you can choose more than one):

Happy   Sad   Angry   Confused   Calm
Missing Nana   Loved

Then write or draw about your feelings below

Reflection 2

Reflect on Your Drawing

2. What did you draw?

Todays Date:

My Feelings Today

Circle how you're feeling right now (you can choose more than one):

Happy   Sad   Angry   Confused   Calm
Missing Grandma   Loved

Then write or draw about your feelings below

Reflection 3

Colors and Shapes

3. What do the colors and shapes mean to you?

Todays Date:

My Feelings Today

Circle how you're feeling right now (you can choose more than one):

Happy　　Sad　　Angry　　Confused　　Calm
Missing Granma　　Loved

Then write or draw about your feelings below

Reflection 4

Painting Memories

4. Paint a picture of a happy memory with your Gran.

Todays Date:

My Feelings Today

Circle how you're feeling right now (you can choose more than one):

Happy   Sad   Angry   Confused   Calm
Missing Gran   Loved

Then write or draw about your feelings below

Reflection 5

Moment Reflection

5. What moment did you choose?

Todays Date:

My Feelings Today

Circle how you're feeling right now (you can choose more than one):

Happy   Sad   Angry   Confused   Calm
Missing Granny   Loved

Then write or draw about your feelings below

Reflection 6

Paint It

6. How did it feel to paint it?

Todays Date:

My Feelings Today

Circle how you're feeling right now (you can choose more than one):

Happy   Sad   Angry   Confused   Calm
Missing Nonna   Loved

Then write or draw about your feelings below

Reflection 7

Crafting a Tribute

7. Create a small tribute-this could be a card, a picture, a decorated memory box, or a poem.

Todays Date:

My Feelings Today

Circle how you're feeling right now (you can choose more than one):

Happy   Sad   Angry   Confused   Calm
Missing Nana   Loved

Then write or draw about your feelings below

Reflection 8

What Did you Make?

8. What did you make and why?

Todays Date:

My Feelings Today

Circle how you're feeling right now (you can choose more than one):

Happy   Sad   Angry   Confused   Calm
Missing Nonna   Loved

Then write or draw about your feelings below

Reflection 9

9. If you could tell your Gran one thing today, what would it be?

Draw it or write about it

Todays Date:

My Feelings Today

Circle how you're feeling right now (you can choose more than one):

 Happy   Sad   Angry   Confused   Calm
Missing Gran   Loved

Then write or draw about your feelings below

Reflection 10

10. How did it help you remember your Granma?

Todays Date:

My Feelings Today

Circle how you're feeling right now (you can choose more than one):

Happy   Sad   Angry   Confused   Calm
Missing Granma   Loved

Then write or draw about your feelings below

Reflection 11

11. Journaling Time--------------Activity: Write a letter to your Nan.

Tell her what you miss and what you remember.

Todays Date:

My Feelings Today

Circle how you're feeling right now (you can choose more than one):

Happy   Sad   Angry   Confused   Calm
Missing Nan   Loved

Then write or draw about your feelings below

Reflection 12

12. How did you feel before writing the letter?

How do you feel now?

Todays Date:

My Feelings Today

Circle how you're feeling right now (you can choose more than one):

Happy   Sad   Angry   Confused   Calm
Missing Gran   Loved

Then write or draw about your feelings below

Sharing Stories from the Heart

Chapter 5 - Encourages reflection, creativity, and emotional expressions

In this chapter, we'll explore how stories — both the ones we read and the ones we tell — can help our hearts feel lighter after losing someone we love, like our Grandmother. Books can be like a comforting friend, showing us that other people have felt sad and confused too, and that it's okay to miss someone very much.

You'll learn ways to write your own stories, keep a journal full of memories, and even share those stories with people you trust.

We'll also talk about how being quiet in nature or sitting in a peaceful spot can help you feel calm when your feelings feel too big.

Every memory, every word, and every picture you create is a way to keep your Grandmama's love shining bright inside you — like a warm hug that never goes away.

BooksThat Help Us Feel Understood

Books can be like gentle friends when we're feeling sad. Reading about characters who are missing someone special, like their Oma, helps us feel less alone. These stories often show us that it's okay to feel a mix of emotions—like sadness, anger, or even confusion—when someone we love is no longer here. Seeing how others move through grief can help us find new ways to understand our own feelings.

Telling Your Own Story

Sometimes, it helps to tell our own stories too. Writing about our Granny, or drawing pictures that remind us of her, can turn our feelings into something beautiful. Maybe you remember her warm hugs or the way she smiled when she saw you. Putting those memories into a story, poem, or picture lets us keep a part of her close, even if she isn't with us anymore.

Journaling from the Heart

A special journal can be a safe place for your thoughts and memories. You can write about your day, draw something that reminds you of your Nan, or even write her a letter. This journal becomes a little treasure chest that you can open whenever you miss her, filled with words and images that come straight from your heart.

Sharing with Others

Joining a support group or sharing with a trusted friend can also help. When we talk with others who have lost someone they love, we learn that it's okay to cry, to laugh, or just to listen. Sharing stories in a circle of understanding hearts can lighten the sadness and remind us that we are not alone.

Finding Calm in the Quiet

And when the feelings get too big, simple things—like taking deep breaths, sitting quietly in a peaceful place, or spending time outdoors—can bring calm to your heart. Nature has a way of reminding us that everything changes, and that healing, like growing, takes time.

Holding On Through Stories

Each story we tell, each picture we draw, is a way of holding onto love. By remembering our Nonna and sharing what's in our hearts, we carry her with us in a way that never fades.

Reflection 1

Sharing Stories from the Heart

1. My Nana, My Memory

Write or draw another favorite memory of your Nonna.

Todays Date:

My Feelings Today

Circle how you're feeling right now (you can choose more than one):

 Happy   Sad   Angry   Confused   Calm
Missing Nana   Loved

Then write or draw about your feelings below

Reflection 2

2. What made it special?

Write it or draw it below

Todays Date:

My Feelings Today

Circle how you're feeling right now (you can choose more than one):

Happy Sad Angry Confused Calm
Missing Nana Loved

Then write or draw about your feelings below

Or draw here:

Reflection 3

A Letter to Granny

3. Imagine you could send a letter to your Granny. You can tell her what you've been up to, how you feel, or what you miss most.

What would you like to tell her today?

Dear Granny,

Love,

_____ (Your Name)

Todays Date:

My Feelings Today

Circle how you're feeling right now (you can choose more than one):

Happy   Sad   Angry   Confused   Calm
Missing Nana   Loved

Then write or draw about your feelings below

Reflection 4

Storytime Feelings

4. Think of a book or story you've read about someone who was sad or missed someone.

What did you learn from their story?

Book or Story Name:

What I learned:

What did the characters do to feel better?

Todays Date:

My Feelings Today

Circle how you're feeling right now (you can choose more than one):

Happy   Sad   Angry   Confused   Calm
Missing Nana   Loved

Then write or draw about your feelings below

Reflection 5

Create From the Heart

. Choose one way to show how you're feeling today:

☐ Draw a picture

☐ Write a poem

☐ Make a mini comic

☐ Create a simple craft (like a heart or memory star)

Todays Date:

My Feelings Today

Circle how you're feeling right now (you can choose more than one):

Happy   Sad   Angry   Confused   Calm
Missing Nana   Loved

Then write or draw about your feelings below

Reflection 6

Quiet Moments

6. Circle the things you like to do when you need to feel calm or remember your Granma:

Go outside   Draw   Read a book   Take deep breaths   Listen to music   Write

Other:

Todays Date:

My Feelings Today

Circle how you're feeling right now (you can choose more than one):

 Happy   Sad   Angry   Confused   Calm
Missing Nana   Loved

Then write or draw about your feelings below

Reflection 7

Make Your Own Story

7. Let's create your own story about Gran. It can be happy, sad, funny, or all of those.

Start your story below:

Title:

Once upon a time...

Todays Date:

My Feelings Today

Circle how you're feeling right now (you can choose more than one):

Happy   Sad   Angry   Confused   Calm
Missing Nana   Loved

Then write or draw about your feelings below

Journaling for Kids

Chapter 6

In this chapter, we'll discover how writing and drawing can help you feel closer to your Nanna, even though she isn't here the same way anymore. Sometimes, talking about our feelings can feel too hard, but when we write them down or draw them, it's like letting our hearts breathe.

We'll explore how to make your own journal or memory book, where you can tell stories, write letters, or draw pictures about your Gran. You'll see how each word or picture is a way to hold onto her love, like a secret hug that lasts forever.

This chapter will help you find small ways to feel better when you're sad, remember the good times, and keep your Gran's spark shining brightly inside you.

Writing from the Heart

Sometimes, our feelings are so big, it's hard to find the right words to say them out loud. That's where journaling can help. Journaling is like talking to a trusted friend—only this friend is your notebook. When you write or draw about your Granma, you are giving your feelings a place to rest, to be seen, and to be understood.

You might start by answering gentle prompts like:

- What is your happiest memory with your Granny?

- What do you wish you could tell her right now?

- What makes you feel close to her?

You can draw, doodle, write poems, or just scribble your thoughts. It doesn't have to be perfect. What matters is that it comes from your heart. Each page is a step toward healing, a small way to carry her love with you.

Drawing Your Feelings

If talking is hard, and writing feels tricky, then let your colors do the speaking. Drawing your feelings can be like opening a window in your heart. Use crayons, pencils, or paints. Let your hand move however it wants. Maybe you'll draw her favorite flower or the smile you remember so well. Maybe your picture will be full of colors that match how you feel inside.

You could even start a "Nonna Memory Book," a journal filled with pictures and notes just for her. Each page is like a hug you send her way. This book becomes your special place, where your love for her can keep growing.

Reflection and Healing

As time goes by, your journal might help you notice how your feelings change. Some days might be full of tears. Others might bring smiles. That's okay. Every feeling is important.

You can also use your journal to explore questions like:

- What do I miss most about my Nana?

- What would I like to do in her memory?

- What makes me feel peaceful when I'm sad?

You might want to share your journal with someone you trust, or keep it all to yourself. Either way, journaling is a gentle way to care for your heart. It helps you see that you are strong, even on the hardest days. And through your words and pictures, you keep your Granny's love shining brightly in your life.

Reflection 1

1. What is another favorite memory with your Gran?

You can write it down or draw it below

Todays Date:

My Feelings Today

Circle how you're feeling right now (you can choose more than one):

Happy   Sad   Angry   Confused   Calm
Missing Nana   Loved

Then write or draw about your feelings below

Reflection 2

2. How do you feel when you think about your Nana?

Write it down or draw it below

Todays Date:

My Feelings Today

Circle how you're feeling right now (you can choose more than one):

Happy   Sad   Angry   Confused   Calm
Missing Nana   Loved

Then write or draw about your feelings below

Reflection 3

3. What else would you like to say to your Granny if you could talk to her right now?

Write it down or draw it below

Todays Date:

My Feelings Today

Circle how you're feeling right now (you can choose more than one):

Happy   Sad   Angry   Confused   Calm
Missing Nana   Loved

Then write or draw about your feelings below

Reflection 4

4. Draw or write about another special moment you shared with your Gran

Write it down or draw it below

Todays Date:

My Feelings Today

Circle how you're feeling right now (you can choose more than one):

Happy   Sad   Angry   Confused   Calm
Missing Nana   Loved

Then write or draw about your feelings below

Reflection 5

5. What do you miss most about your Oma?

Write it down or draw it below

Todays Date:

My Feelings Today

Circle how you're feeling right now (you can choose more than one):

Happy   Sad   Angry   Confused   Calm
Missing Oma   Loved

Then write or draw about your feelings below

Reflection 6

6. What makes you feel better when you are feeling sad?

Write it down or draw it below

Todays Date:

My Feelings Today

Circle how you're feeling right now (you can choose more than one):

Happy   Sad   Angry   Confused   Calm
Missing Gran   Loved

Then write or draw about your feelings below

Reflection 7

7. What is something special you can do to remember your Granny today?

Write it down or draw it below

Todays Date:

My Feelings Today

Circle how you're feeling right now (you can choose more than one):

Happy   Sad   Angry   Confused   Calm
Missing Granny   Loved

Then write or draw about your feelings below

Reflection 8

8. Write a short story or draw a comic about you and your Nonna having an adventure.

Write it down or draw it below

Todays Date:

My Feelings Today

Circle how you're feeling right now (you can choose more than one):

Happy   Sad   Angry   Confused   Calm
Missing Oma   Loved

Then write or draw about your feelings below

Reflection 9

9. Make a list of five things your Granny loved

Write it down or draw it below

Todays Date:

My Feelings Today

Circle how you're feeling right now (you can choose more than one):

Happy   Sad   Angry   Confused   Calm
Missing Grandma   Loved

Then write or draw about your feelings below

Reflection 10

10. How can you keep your Gran's memory close to your heart every day?

Todays Date:

My Feelings Today

Circle how you're feeling right now (you can choose more than one):

Happy   Sad   Angry   Confused   Calm
Missing Gran   Loved

Then write or draw about your feelings below

Comfort in Community

Chapter 7

In this chapter, you'll learn about something called a support group. It might sound like a big word, but really, it's just a group of caring people—kids and adults—who come together to talk about their feelings. When you're missing your Grandmother, it can feel like you're carrying a heavy backpack of emotions all by yourself. A support group is a place where you can put that backpack down for a while, share your thoughts, and hear from others who understand.

Together, you'll explore ways to feel a little better, like making art, writing letters, or even just talking. You'll see that you're not alone in your sadness, and there are kind friends who can help. In this chapter, we'll discover how sharing, listening, and creating can help your heart feel lighter, and remind you that healing doesn't have to happen alone

What Is a Support Group?

When our Nana, passes away, it can feel like we're carrying heavy emotions all by ourselves. But we don't have to go through grief alone. A support group is a special place where kids can gather and talk about their feelings. In this safe and caring space, everyone understands what it's like to miss someone.

You might meet kids who feel just like you—sad, confused, or even a little angry. Sharing your story and hearing theirs can help your heart feel lighter. It's comforting to know that you're not alone.

Sharing Feelings Through Art and Stories

In support groups, there are often creative ways to express feelings. You might draw a picture of your Granny, make a memory craft, or tell a story about a fun time you shared together. These activities help you show your emotions in ways that feel natural, especially when words are hard to find.

You could also read books about other kids who've lost someone special. Their stories might help you understand your own feelings better, and even remind you of your Gran in a comforting way.

The Power of Journaling

Writing in a journal can also be part of support group time—or as previously mentioned, something you do on your own. You can write letters to your Granny, draw how you feel, or keep a list of happy memories. Journaling gives you a private, safe place to explore your thoughts. And if you want to, you can share it with others, too.

Talking With Friends Who Understand

Talking with other kids who are going through something similar can make a big difference. You might laugh together, cry together, or just listen. These friendships can bring comfort and help you feel understood. You'll learn that it's okay to feel whatever you're feeling—and that healing takes time, but it's easier when we're not alone.

Finding Calm Together

Support groups often include relaxing activities too. Breathing exercises, gentle stretches, or simply sitting quietly can help calm your heart when your feelings feel too big. Being with others who care can bring peace to your day, even if just for a little while.

Healing as a Group

Grief is something we all experience differently, but support groups remind us that we don't have to face it by ourselves. Whether we talk, create, read, or simply sit with others, being part of a caring community helps us feel stronger. We learn, together, how to carry our love for our Grandma forward in a way that brings comfort and connection.

Reflection 1

Todays Date:

1. My Feelings Today

Circle how you're feeling right now (you can choose more than one):

Happy   Sad   Angry   Confused   Calm
Missing Gran   Loved

Then write or draw about your feelings below

Reflection 2

Picture of a Memory

Draw a picture or write about something you remember doing with your Grandmother that made you feel happy or loved.

Write it down or draw it below

Todays Date:

My Feelings Today

Circle how you're feeling right now (you can choose more than one):

Happy   Sad   Angry   Confused   Calm
Missing Nana   Loved

Then write or draw about your feelings below

Todays Date:

My Feelings Today

Circle how you're feeling right now (you can choose more than one):

Happy   Sad   Angry   Confused   Calm
Missing Nana   Loved

Then write or draw about your feelings below

Reflection 3

My Safe Sharing Space

Todays Date:

Who do you feel comfortable talking to about your feelings?

Why do you feel safe with them?

Write it down or draw it below

My Feelings Today

Circle how you're feeling right now (you can choose more than one):

Happy   Sad   Angry   Confused   Calm
Missing Granny   Loved

Then write or draw about your feelings below

Reflection 4

A Message to a Friend in My Group

Write a kind note you could give to another kid in your group or class who might be feeling sad.

Todays Date:

Dear friend,

From, _____

My Feelings Today

Circle how you're feeling right now (you can choose more than one):

 Happy   Sad   Angry   Confused   Calm
Missing Grandma   Loved

Then write or draw about your feelings below

Reflection 5

Calm and Quiet Time

What helps you feel peaceful when your heart feels heavy?

☐ Taking deep breaths   ☐ Drawing or coloring   ☐ Going for a walk

☐ Talking to someone I trust   ☐ Writing in my journal   Other: _____

Write it down or draw it below

My Feelings Today

Circle how you're feeling right now (you can choose more than one):

Happy   Sad   Angry   Confused   Calm
Missing Gran   Loved

Then write or draw about your feelings below

Finding Calm Inside

Chapter 8

In this chapter, we're going to learn about ways to help your heart feel a little calmer when you miss your Grandma. Sometimes, big feelings can swirl around like a wild storm inside you. That's where breathing, mindfulness, and creating a calm space come in.

Breathing exercises are like pressing a magic pause button for your feelings, helping you feel safe and steady. Mindful moments can help you notice how you feel right now, without rushing or hiding from those feelings. And a calm space is a cozy spot that belongs just to you—where you can rest, remember, and breathe.

Together, these ideas are like gentle tools you can keep in your pocket. Whenever the sadness feels too big, or you just need a break, you can use them to feel stronger and remind yourself that your Nana's love is still with you, no matter what.

Breathing Exercises

When we miss our Granma, our big emotions may feel as if they swirling inside us. Breathing exercises can help us slow down, feel safe, and bring a little peace to our hearts.

One fun way to calm down is to imagine you have a balloon in your belly. Breathe in deeply through your nose and picture the balloon slowly filling with air. Then breathe out gently through your mouth, like letting the air out softly. This can help your body and your mind relax.

Another way is the "flower and candle" method. Pretend you're smelling a beautiful flower as you breathe in, and then blow out a candle as you breathe out. These simple movements help remind us we are safe, and that it's okay to feel however we're feeling.

You can do these exercises anywhere—at home, school, or even while walking outside. Breathing is something we always carry with us, like a quiet superpower that helps us find calm when we need it most.

Mindful Moments

Mindfulness means paying close attention to how we feel right now. When we remember our Grandmother, we might feel happy, sad, or something in between. Taking a mindful moment helps us notice those feelings without rushing past them.

Nature is also a wonderful place to be mindful. Sitting quietly under a tree, listening to birds, or watching clouds can help you feel peaceful. Even a short walk can remind you that the world is full of calm and beauty, just like the love you carry for your nana.

Creating a Calm Space

Having your own calm space can be comforting. It can be a corner of your room, a small reading nook, or even a spot in the garden. Fill it with things that make you feel safe—like a soft blanket, a photo of your nana, your favorite book, or some art supplies.

In your calm space, you can draw, write, or just sit quietly with your thoughts. You might create a memory box or decorate your space with drawings of things that remind you of your nana. It's your special place to relax and feel connected to her.

You might also want to read books in your calm space—stories about kids who are going through similar things. These stories can show that it's okay to feel a lot of different emotions, and that healing takes time.

Sometimes, it helps to invite a friend, parent, or sibling to your calm space. Talking, sharing memories, or just sitting together can bring comfort. Even being quiet together can remind you that you're not alone.

And as previously mentioned, you can practice mindfulness by being creative—drawing a picture, painting, or crafting something that reminds you of your nana. These activities let your feelings out gently and help your heart feel lighter.

Journaling is another mindful activity. You can write about your day, your favorite memories with nana, or how you're feeling. A journal is like a private friend who listens to every word without interrupting.

Reflection 1

Try a Breathing Exercise

1. Pick one of these and try it for one minute:

☐ Balloon Belly Breathing ☐ Flower and Candle Breathing

How did you feel before?

How did you feel after?

Write it down or draw it below

Todays Date:

My Feelings Today

Circle how you're feeling right now (you can choose more than one):

Happy   Sad   Angry   Confused   Calm
Missing Nana   Loved

Then write or draw about your feelings below

Reflection 2

Create a Memory Drawing

Draw something that reminds you of a special time with your Gran.

Todays Date:

My Feelings Today

Circle how you're feeling right now (you can choose more than one):

Happy   Sad   Angry   Confused   Calm
Missing Gran   Loved

Then write or draw about your feelings below

Reflection 3

What's in My Calm Space?

3. Write or draw 3 things you would put in your calm space and why:

1.

2.

3.

Todays Date:

My Feelings Today

Circle how you're feeling right now (you can choose more than one):

Happy   Sad   Angry   Confused   Calm
Missing Nan   Loved

Then write or draw about your feelings below

Reflection 4

Mindful Moment Journal Prompt

4.Take a moment to sit quietly and notice how you're feeling.

Write or draw about what's in your heart right now.

Todays Date:

My Feelings Today

Circle how you're feeling right now (you can choose more than one):

Happy   Sad   Angry   Confused   Calm
Missing Granny   Loved

Then write or draw about your feelings below

Reflection 5

My Comfort Plan

5. What can you do next time you feel over-whelmed or really miss your Nonna?

☐ Take deep breaths

☐ Sit in my calm space

☐ Draw or write about my feelings

☐ Talk to someone I trust

Other

Todays Date:

My Feelings Today

Circle how you're feeling right now (you can choose more than one):

Happy   Sad   Angry   Confused   Calm
Missing Nana   Loved

Then write or draw about your feelings below

Honoring Nana Through Memories

Chapter 9

In this chapter, we will discover how to keep your Nana's love alive in sweet and special ways. Sometimes, when someone we love is no longer with us, we want to find ways to remember them that feel comforting and peaceful.

Planting a memory tree can help you create a living reminder of your Granny. Every leaf and branch becomes part of your story together. A memory box is like a tiny treasure chest where you can keep all the pieces of your love—pictures, letters, or little things that make you think of her. And celebrating your Granny's life with family and friends reminds you that the happy moments you shared can keep shining, even on the hardest days.

These ideas are here to help you feel connected, to honor your memories, and to remind you that love never truly goes away—it just grows in new ways, just like you.

Planting a Memory Tree

Planting a memory tree is a gentle and meaningful way to remember your Oma. As the tree grows, it becomes a symbol of your love and the time you shared. It gives you a special place to visit, sit quietly, and think about the happy memories you have of her.

To get started, you'll need a small tree or plant, some soil, and maybe a few special decorations—like painted stones, ribbons, or a sign with her name. Choose a place that feels peaceful to you. It might be your backyard, a sunny spot in the park, or even a pot on your windowsill.

As you plant the tree, think about your favorite moments with your Grandmother—her laugh, the stories she told, or something kind she always said. Talking to her in your heart while you plant can be a comforting way to stay close.

Once it's in the ground, you can make the space around it feel even more special. Add small decorations or things that remind you of her. Invite others to join you, share memories, and help create a place of love and remembrance.

Over time, your tree will grow—just like your memories. It will always be there to remind you of how deeply you are loved.

Crafting a Memory Box

A memory box is like a little treasure chest for your heart. It holds the pieces of your love and helps you feel connected to your Gran even though she isn't physically here.

Start by choosing a box that feels right to you. It could be simple or decorated—whatever feels special. Fill it with things that remind you of her: photos, small objects, drawings, letters, or poems.

Each item you place inside tells a story. You might remember baking together, walking in the garden, or sharing hugs. These memories bring her closer and help you keep her spirit alive in your heart.

Decorate your box with colors, words, or pictures that make you think of her. This is your own way of honoring the love you shared. You can return to your box anytime—when you're sad, or just when you want to feel near her.

Celebrating Nonna's Life

Remembering your Granny doesn't always have to feel sad. You can also celebrate all the happiness she brought to your life.

Think about the things that made her special—her favorite song, the way she smiled, or the things she loved to do. You can create artwork that shows a favorite memory, or write a letter to her in your journal.

Reading books about other kids who've lost someone can help you see that you're not alone. These stories can comfort you and give you new ideas for honoring your Granma in your own way.

You might also want to gather with family or friends for a special day of remembrance. You could plant flowers, share stories, or cook her favorite meal together. These little celebrations help keep her memory alive and bring a sense of joy back into your heart.

Grief is about love—and celebrating your Oma's life is a way to let that love keep growing.

Reflection 1

My Memory Tree Plan

1. If I planted a memory tree for my Nana, I would choose:

Type of tree or plant:

_____

Where I'd plant it:

_____

One memory I'd think about while planting:

Todays Date:

My Feelings Today

Circle how you're feeling right now (you can choose more than one):

Happy Sad Angry Confused Calm
Missing Nanny Loved

Then write or draw about your feelings below

Reflection 2

My Memory Box Ideas

2. What would you place in your memory box? Write or draw 3 items and what they mean to you:

1.

2.

3.

Todays Date:

My Feelings Today

Circle how you're feeling right now (you can choose more than one):

Happy   Sad   Angry   Confused   Calm
Missing Granny   Loved

Then write or draw about your feelings below

Reflection 3

Create and Celebrate

3. Draw or describe something you could do to celebrate your Gran's life.

It could be a picture, a meal, or a favorite song.

Todays Date:

My Feelings Today

Circle how you're feeling right now (you can choose more than one):

Happy   Sad   Angry   Confused   Calm
Missing Gran   Loved

Then write or draw about your feelings below

Reflection 4

A Letter to My Granny

Dear Granny,

I miss you. One thing I really loved about you was...

Love, _____

Todays Date:

My Feelings Today

Circle how you're feeling right now (you can choose more than one):

Happy   Sad   Angry   Confused   Calm
Missing Granny   Loved

Then write or draw about your feelings below

Reflection 5

My Special Day Plan

5. If I created a day to remember Nan, it would include:

☐ Sharing stories   ☐ Making her favorite food   ☐ Planting something

☐ Drawing together   ☐ Reading a memory book   Other: _____

Write about it or draw it below

Todays Date:

My Feelings Today

Circle how you're feeling right now (you can choose more than one):

Happy Sad Angry Confused Calm
Missing Nana Loved

Then write or draw about your feelings below

Learning About Feelings

Chapter 10

In this chapter, we're going to explore why sharing our feelings is so important — especially when we're missing our Nana. Sometimes, it can feel really hard to put our feelings into words. You might feel worried, sad, or even angry, and that's okay. All feelings are welcome here.

You'll learn gentle ways to talk about what's in your heart. That might be through words, art, storytelling, or even fun role-playing games. You might share a memory at dinner, or talk to a trusted grown-up about something that makes you miss your Granny. Each time you speak or show how you feel, it helps your heart feel a little bit lighter.

This chapter will help you remember that feelings aren't wrong or scary — they're just your heart's way of telling its story. And you don't have to go through it alone. Whether you talk with your family, friends, or other kids who understand, you'll see that you're never alone with your feelings.

Talking About Feelings

Sometimes, talking about how we feel is the hardest part. It can be tricky to explain what's happening in our hearts, especially when we're grieving. But it's important to remember that your feelings matter—and sharing them helps you heal.

There are many ways to talk about your emotions. You can use words, pictures, or even stories. You might talk about your Nan during dinner, or share a memory with a friend at school. You could say, "I miss her today," or "This reminds me of her." Every time you speak your feelings, you're letting them out so they don't stay stuck inside.

Art can help too. In workshops or at home, you can paint or draw something that shows how you're feeling. Maybe it's a rainbow for hope, or a stormy sky to show sadness. There's no wrong way to create—it's all about what your heart wants to say.

Reading stories with family or friends can open the door to important conversations. If you find a character who reminds you of your Granny, talk about that connection. These moments bring comfort and help others understand what you're going through.

Role-Playing Emotions

Sometimes the best way to understand a feeling is to act it out. Role-playing is a fun and safe way to explore different emotions, especially those connected to grief.

You might play a game where you pretend to talk to your Grandmother, or you could act out how you feel when you're missing her. Maybe you're feeling frustrated, or maybe you want to share a memory. When you role-play with someone you trust, it helps your body and heart work together to understand your feelings.

Art can also be part of this. Use modeling clay or puppets to create scenes that express your emotions. You might make a sculpture of your Nonna's house or create a comic strip about a happy memory. These playful activities help your emotions feel lighter.

And as previously mentioned, books, journaling, and support groups also help during this time. Reading stories about other children who've lost someone reminds you that grief is something many people feel. And keeping a journal lets you reflect quietly and safely on what you're going through.

Support groups bring kids together to share their stories. You can learn from each other, talk about your feelings, and find comfort in knowing you're not alone. These moments help you feel stronger and more supported as you heal.

Reflection 1

Color My Feeling

1. Draw a big heart. Inside it, use colors to show what you're feeling today.

2. Write what each color means next to it.

3. Color: _____ =

   _____

4. Color: _____ =

   _____

5. Color: _____ =

   _____

Todays Date:

My Feelings Today

Circle how you're feeling right now (you can choose more than one):

Happy   Sad   Angry   Confused   Calm
Missing Nonna   Loved

Then write or draw about your feelings below

Reflection 2

What I Want to Say

2. If you could tell your Granma something right now, what would it be?

Write it or draw it below

Todays Date:

My Feelings Today

Circle how you're feeling right now (you can choose more than one):

Happy   Sad   Angry   Confused   Calm
Missing Granma   Loved

Then write or draw about your feelings below

Reflection 3

Book Connection

3. Think of a story or book you've read about someone who lost a loved one.

Book title:

What part of the story reminded you of your Nan or your feelings?

Todays Date:

My Feelings Today

Circle how you're feeling right now (you can choose more than one):

Happy   Sad   Angry   Confused   Calm
Missing Nan   Loved

Then write or draw about your feelings below

Reflection 4

Talking Practice

4. Write down or draw one way you could share how you're feeling with someone you trust.

Who   would   you   talk   to?
_____

What   would   you   say   or   draw?
_____

Todays Date:

My Feelings Today

Circle how you're feeling right now (you can choose more than one):

Happy   Sad   Angry   Confused   Calm
Missing Nana   Loved

Then write or draw about your feelings below

Reflection 5

Act It Out

5. Choose one feeling and show it through an action:

☐ Joy – act out a happy memory

☐ Sadness – show what helps you feel better

☐ Love – show how you remember your Gran-ma

☐ Confusion – ask a question you wonder about

Draw or write about what you acted out:

Todays Date:

My Feelings Today

Circle how you're feeling right now (you can choose more than one):

Happy   Sad   Angry   Confused   Calm
Missing Granma   Loved

Then write or draw about your feelings below

Grief Games and Gentle Sharing

Chapter 11

In this chapter, we're going to discover that talking about losing someone we love — like your Granma — doesn't have to be scary or lonely. Sometimes it can feel too big or too hard to put into words. That's why creative and fun activities can help.

When we play games, make art, or share stories, it gives our hearts a chance to speak in gentle ways. These activities can remind us of happy memories and help us feel connected to our Gran, even though she isn't here in the same way anymore.

You'll find ideas for drawing, painting, sharing, and even acting out your feelings with trusted friends or family. There are no wrong answers, and no one way to heal — just kind ways to remember the love you still carry inside.

Let's explore together, one gentle step at a time.

Fun Ways to Talk About Loss

Talking about losing your Oma can be hard. But sometimes, playful and creative activities can make it easier to open up. Games, art, and stories can gently help us share our thoughts and remember her with love.

You might start by drawing or painting something that reminds you of her—her favorite flower, a cozy chair she loved, or a happy memory you shared. Creating art helps your feelings come out in a quiet, safe way.

You could even create a simple memorial activity—like planting a flower, making a scrapbook, or just spending time in a quiet place that reminds you of her. These small acts help keep your Granny's memory close in a comforting way.

Games for Sharing Feelings

Games can be a fun way to talk about hard things. When you're feeling sad or unsure, playing together can help your feelings come out more easily.

One simple game is **"Memory Sharing."** Each person takes turns saying a happy memory about their Nana while others listen and support them. It feels good to talk about the good times and to be heard by others who care.

Another game is **"Feelings Charades."** You act out emotions like sadness, joy, or anger without using words, and others guess what you're feeling. It helps everyone learn to notice and understand different feelings in a fun way.

You can also create something together—like a big collage where everyone adds a picture or word about their feelings. Working as a group can help you feel connected and remind you that you're not alone.

Reading and talking about stories with characters who've lost someone can also be a great game. You can take turns sharing your favorite part or talking about how it made you feel. These stories open doors to deeper understanding.

Grief games are not just about playing—they're a kind and creative way to feel your feelings and heal with others.

Creative Icebreakers

Sometimes starting a conversation feels scary. But creative icebreakers can help you feel comfortable sharing about your Nonna and listening to others too.

One fun idea is to **draw a memory.** Everyone draws a picture of something they remember about their Grandma. Then you can share your drawing and talk about the story behind it.

You might also try **story circles,** where each person shares a short story or moment they loved with their Granny. Hearing others talk about their memories helps you feel less alone.

For a writing icebreaker, you can start with a simple journal prompt:

"What do you miss most about your Nana?"

Then you can share your answers if you feel ready. This helps everyone understand each other's feelings a little better.

Spending time in nature can also help start conversations. You could take a short walk together, pick up leaves or stones that remind you of her, and then use them in a group art project. Being outside can make it easier to talk and feel calm at the same time.

Even playing light-hearted games about feelings can help everyone feel ready to share. These little icebreakers open the door to healing, connection, and remembering the love you still carry inside.

Reflection 1

Draw a Memory Game

1. Draw a special memory of your Nan that makes you smile.

Under your drawing, write a sentence about what's happening in the picture.

Todays Date:

My Feelings Today

Circle how you're feeling right now (you can choose more than one):

Happy   Sad   Angry   Confused   Calm
Missing Granma   Loved

Then write or draw about your feelings below

Reflection 2

Feelings Charades

2. Circle some emotions you might act out in a game of feelings charades:

Happy   Sad   Angry   Confused
Loved   Excited

Pick one. How would you act it out without using words?

Todays Date:

My Feelings Today

Circle how you're feeling right now (you can choose more than one):

Happy   Sad   Angry   Confused   Calm
Missing Granmama   Loved

Then write or draw about your feelings below

Reflection 3

Movie Reflection

3. Think of a movie that you've watched about someone who lost a loved one.

Movie title:

What part of the story reminded you of your Oma?

Todays Date:

My Feelings Today

Circle how you're feeling right now (you can choose more than one):

Happy   Sad   Angry   Confused   Calm
Missing Oma   Loved

Then write or draw about your feelings below

Reflection 4

4. Write or draw a response to this prompt:

"Something I miss about my Nan is..."

Todays Date:

My Feelings Today

Circle how you're feeling right now (you can choose more than one):

Happy   Sad   Angry   Confused   Calm
Missing Nan   Loved

Then write or draw about your feelings below

Reflection 5

5. What would you bring back from a nature walk that reminds you of your Grandma?

☐ A flower   ☐ A leaf   ☐ A stone   ☐ A feather   Other:

What would you do with it?

Write about it or draw it

Todays Date:

My Feelings Today

Circle how you're feeling right now (you can choose more than one):

Happy Sad Angry Confused Calm Missing Grandma Loved

Then write or draw about your feelings below

Nature and Healing

Chapter 12

In this chapter, we're going to discover how nature can help us feel better when we're missing our Nonna. The world outside is full of gentle sounds, colors, and peaceful places that can bring calm to your heart. Whether you're taking a walk in the park, planting flowers, or just sitting under a tree, being outdoors can remind you of all the love and happy memories you shared.

We'll talk about nature walks, memory gardens, and other ways you can feel close to your Gran even though she isn't here in the same way. These activities are simple, kind, and full of hope—just like the love you carry for her.

Let's step outside together and see how the beauty of nature can help your heart heal.

Exploring the Outdoors

Nature is full of peaceful places that can help your heart feel lighter when you're missing your Oma. Taking a walk in the park, listening to birds sing, or watching the leaves flutter in the wind can bring a sense of calm. Being outside can remind you of happy times and make you feel connected to her in a quiet, gentle way.

One beautiful idea is to create a **memory garden**. You can plant flowers, decorate stones, or even draw pictures of your nana's favorite things and place them in a special outdoor spot. As you care for your garden, you can think about her love and all the joy she brought into your life.

Or go on a **nature scavenger hunt**. Look for things like a soft feather, a smooth rock, or a colorful leaf. With each item you find, take a quiet moment to think about your Gran. Nature can help you remember her in simple, thoughtful ways.

You might also have a **picnic** in a place that reminds you of her. Bring a snack she loved, and share stories with someone close to you. You can even bring a journal to write or draw about how you're feeling. Spending time out-doors can make remembering her feel warm and comforting.

Nature Walks for Reflection

Walking in nature is a lovely way to think about your feelings and remember your Grandmother. As you step outside, notice the sky, the trees, and all the small sounds around you. These moments can help you slow down and feel more peaceful inside.

During your walk, you can talk about mem-ories that make you smile—like something funny she said, or a game you used to play together. You can also just walk quietly and think. Nature gives you space to feel however you need to feel—whether that's happy, sad, or somewhere in between.

You might want to collect leaves or small stones during your walk and turn them into a little art project. You could create a picture or a decoration in her honor. These small projects can turn your feelings into something beautiful.

While you walk, try taking slow, deep breaths. Notice how the air feels, the sounds around you, or how the sun feels on your face. This practice is called **mindfulness**, and it helps you stay connected to the present moment. Mindfulness in nature can help calm your thoughts and gently support your healing.

Connecting with Nature

Nature is a quiet friend who listens and comforts. When you spend time outdoors, it can feel like the world is wrapping you in a gentle hug. The wind, the sky, the trees—they remind us that even when things change, love stays with us.

You can honor your Nana by spending time in places she loved or by doing something kind for nature in her memory. Maybe plant a flower, pick up litter at a park, or sit quietly in her favorite spot.

You can even create a **nature journal**, where you write or draw things you see outside that make you think of her. It's a special way to hold onto the connection, even as time moves on.

And remember, you don't have to do this alone. Bring a friend, a parent, or a sibling. Talk about your memories, or just enjoy the peacefulness together. Healing often happens in little moments—and nature is full of them.

Reflection 1

Create Your Memory Garden

1. What would you put in a memory garden for your Gran?

☐ Her favorite flower

☐ A special stone

☐ A drawing of something she loved

☐ A small sign with her name

Other:
_____

Draw your memory garden here

Todays Date:

My Feelings Today

Circle how you're feeling right now (you can choose more than one):

Happy   Sad   Angry   Confused   Calm
Missing Gran   Loved

Then write or draw about your feelings below

Reflection 2

Nature Walk Reflection

2. During a walk outside, what did you see or hear that made you feel peaceful?

Write or draw one memory of your Granny that came to mind:

Todays Date:

My Feelings Today

Circle how you're feeling right now (you can choose more than one):

Happy   Sad   Angry   Confused   Calm
Missing Granny   Loved

Then write or draw about your feelings below

Reflection 3

Nature Scavenger Hunt

3. Check off the things you find in nature that remind you of your Granma:

☐ A smooth rock

☐ A feather

☐ A leaf shaped like a heart

☐ A colorful flower

☐ Something that makes a sound

Other:

Todays Date:

My Feelings Today

Circle how you're feeling right now (you can choose more than one):

Happy   Sad   Angry   Confused   Calm
Missing Granma   Loved

Then write or draw about your feelings below

Reflection 4

My Nature Journal Prompt

4. Finish this sentence in words or drawings:

"When I'm outside, I feel close to my Nana because..."

Todays Date:

My Feelings Today

Circle how you're feeling right now (you can choose more than one):

Happy   Sad   Angry   Confused   Calm
Missing Nana   Loved

Then write or draw about your feelings below

Talking and Listening Together

Chapter 13

In this chapter, we'll explore how talking about grief can help your heart feel a little lighter. When someone as special as your Nana dies, your feelings might feel big and heavy. You might feel sad, worried, angry, or even confused—and that's okay. Sharing those feelings with someone you trust, like a parent, friend, or counselor, can make a big difference.

We'll learn about ways to talk and listen, like telling stories, making art, or joining a group with other kids who have also lost someone. You'll discover how creating a safe space—at home, in nature, or with friends—can help you feel calm and supported.

Remember, there's no wrong way to grieve, and no wrong way to talk about it. Every time you share your memories and feelings, you're honoring your Gran and showing your heart how strong it can be. Let's learn together how talking, listening, and being kind to ourselves can help us heal.

Talking Openly About Grief

Talking about grief isn't always easy. You might feel sad, confused, or even angry—and all of those feelings are okay. Sharing your emotions with someone you trust can help your heart feel lighter, and it can remind you that you're not alone.

Sometimes, it helps to use art to express what you're feeling. You can draw or paint a picture of a favorite memory, or create a special scrapbook with photos and decorations. These pieces of art tell a story of love and help you remember your Nonna in your own unique way.

Telling stories is also a great way to explore your emotions. You can read books about characters who have experienced a loss, or you can write your own story about your Grandmother. These stories help you understand your feelings and show you that others feel them too.

You might also join a group where kids can talk about grief together. These are safe places to share thoughts and memories. Being with others who understand can bring comfort and new ways to heal.

And remember to care for yourself—take deep breaths, rest when you need to, and spend time in nature. Talking about grief, even a little at a time, helps your heart grow stronger and helps you celebrate the love you still carry for your Granny.

Listening to Each Other

When we listen to someone talk about how they feel, we are giving them a gift. And when others listen to us, it helps us feel seen and cared for. After losing your Granny, sharing memories with family and friends can help everyone feel more connected.

You can listen while someone tells a story about your Oma, or you can share your own. Maybe someone remembers a silly joke she told, or how she always made your favorite snack. Talking and listening together helps keep her memory alive.

Art can also help you listen without words. If someone draws a picture that shows their feelings, you can talk about what they created and ask questions. You might even make art together, which opens space for quiet sharing.

Journaling is a gentle way to listen to your own heart. Writing or drawing in a journal helps you understand your feelings and gives you something to share when you're ready.

Mindfulness—like deep breathing or sitting quietly—can help you feel calm and ready to listen. When you listen with your heart, you're showing love and kindness. Together, through listening and talking, you and your family can help each other heal.

Creating a Safe Space for Feelings

When you're grieving, having a safe space to share your feelings is really important. This space could be a cozy corner in your room, a peaceful spot outside, or even a soft chair where you like to sit and think. What matters most is that you feel comfortable there.

In your safe space, you can draw, write, talk, or just be quiet. You can create art about your Nana, or make something that helps you feel close to her. These creative moments help you express what's in your heart—even when it's hard to find the right words.

Reading books or watching movies about other kids who are grieving can also bring comfort. These stories help you feel understood and show you that healing takes time.

You might use a journal in your safe space. Fill it with letters, pictures, or memories about your Granma. You can read it later, share it with someone you trust, or just keep it for yourself.

Being part of a group where kids talk about grief can also feel like a safe space. You can talk, play, or just listen. Everyone understands what you're feeling, and together, you help each other feel stronger.

Creating a space—inside and out—where your feelings are welcome gives your heart the room it needs to heal.

Reflection 1

My Talking Place

1. Where do you feel most comfortable sharing your feelings?

☐ My room

☐ With a friend

☐ In nature

☐ With a parent or caregiver

Other

Why is this your safe space?

Todays Date:

My Feelings Today

Circle how you're feeling right now (you can choose more than one):

Happy   Sad   Angry   Confused   Calm
Missing Oma   Loved

Then write or draw about your feelings below

Reflection 2

Memory Art

Draw or describe a memory of your Nana that you'd like to share with someone.

Todays Date:

My Feelings Today

Circle how you're feeling right now (you can choose more than one):

Happy   Sad   Angry   Confused   Calm
Missing Nana   Loved

Then write or draw about your feelings below

Reflection 3

Story Connection

3. Write the title of a book or story from a movie about loss you've read or watched

Book Title:

What did the character feel that you also feel?

Todays Date:

My Feelings Today

Circle how you're feeling right now (you can choose more than one):

Happy   Sad   Angry   Confused   Calm
Missing Grandma   Loved

Then write or draw about your feelings below

Reflection 4

Listen With Your Heart

4. Think of someone you could listen to today.

Who is it?

What would you say to show them you care?

Todays Date:

My Feelings Today

Circle how you're feeling right now (you can choose more than one):

 Happy   Sad   Angry   Confused   Calm
Missing Granny   Loved

Then write or draw about your feelings below

Reflection 5

Safe Space Checklist

5. Check all the things you'd like in your safe space:

☐ A journal

☐ Art supplies

☐ A cozy blanket

☐ Pictures of Nonna

☐ A favorite book

☐ A place to be quiet

Other:

Todays Date:

My Feelings Today

Circle how you're feeling right now (you can choose more than one):

Happy   Sad   Angry   Confused   Calm
Missing Nonna   Loved

Then write or draw about your feelings below

A Hug That Stays in Our Hearts

Chapter 14

Grief is a journey filled with many different feelings. Sometimes we feel sad, other times we might laugh at a memory, and sometimes we just want to be quiet. In this book, we've walked together through 13 special chapters, each one offering a new way to understand and cope with the loss of someone we love—like our nonna.

We learned that it's okay to feel all kinds of emotions. In **Chapter 1**, we began by exploring how grief feels, and in **Chapter 2**, we discovered that expressing those feelings—through talking, drawing, or writing—can bring comfort. In **Chapter 3**, we remembered that our memories are treasures we can keep close, and in **Chapter 4**, we saw how important it is to share our feelings with people we trust.

In **Chapter 5**, we found that stories and books help us feel less alone, and in **Chapter 6**, we used creative expression to show our emotions in new ways. Then, in **Chapter 7**, we discovered how support groups can bring us together with others who understand.

Chapter 8 taught us how breathing and mindfulness can calm our hearts. In **Chapter 9**, we created memory trees and boxes to celebrate our Gran's life. **Chapter 10** helped us understand emotions more clearly, while **Chapter 11** showed us that games and gentle activities can help us talk about our grief.

In **Chapter 12**, we explored nature and found that the outdoors can be a healing place. And in **Chapter 13**, we learned how important it is to talk and listen within our families, creating safe spaces where everyone can share and heal together.

Each chapter has given us something special—a tool, a story, or a way to remember. And through it all, one thing stays true: the love we have for our nana never goes away. It stays with us, tucked gently in our hearts, like a hug that never fades.

So, as you move forward, carry your memories like stars in your pocket. Let them shine on the days when you miss her most. Talk when you need to, listen with kindness, and take time to breathe, draw, and simply be. You are never alone on this journey—and the love you feel is always, always worth remembering.

Final Reflections

Todays Date:

My Feelings Today

Circle how you're feeling right now (you can choose more than one):

Happy   Sad   Angry   Confused   Calm
Missing Granny   Loved

Then write or draw about your feelings below

Chapter 1: Understanding Grief

What does grief feel like to you?

Chapter 2: Expressing Feelings

How do you like to share your feelings—talking, drawing, writing, or something else?

Chapter 3: Remembering Special Moments

Write or draw one happy memory of your Nana:

Chapter 4: Talking with Someone You Trust

Who do you feel safe talking to when you're feeling sad?

Chapter 5: Learning Through Stories

What book or story helped you feel less alone?

Chapter 6: Creative Ways to Heal

What kind of art have you made to help with your feelings?

Chapter 7: Support from Others

What is something kind someone has said to you in a support group or from a friend?

Chapter 8: Finding Calm

What breathing or mindfulness activity helped you feel better?

Chapter 9: Celebrating Memories

Did you make a memory tree, memory box, or something else?

What did you include in it?

Chapter 10: Learning About Emotions

Which emotion do you now understand better?

Chapter 11: Grief Games

Which game or activity helped you share your feelings in a fun way?

Chapter 12: Nature and Healing

Where in nature do you feel closest to your Gran?

Chapter 13: Talking and Listening with Family

What helps you feel safe when talking with your family?

Chapter 14: A Hug That Stays in Our Hearts

What will you carry in your heart forever about your Nonna?

Gentle Reminders for Grownups

Supporting Grieving Children

Listen More Than You Speak
Children often express grief in small, scattered ways. Be patient and let them talk when they're ready—without pushing for answers or fixing every silence. Simply being present matters more than saying the "right" thing.

Watch for Changes in Behavior
Grieving kids may become quieter, more emotional, or act out in unexpected ways. Gentle routines, extra patience, and comfort

, extra patience, and comfort through play or art   can help them feel safe again.

Create Opportunities to Remember
Encourage memory-making activities like drawing, storytelling, or visiting a special place. These help children process their loss while feeling connected to the person they miss.

Support, Don't Rush
There's no timeline for grief. Some days they may laugh, other days they may cry—and both are normal. Let them go at their own pace, and reassure them that their feelings are okay.

Take Care of Yourself, Too
Children often mirror the emotions of the adults around them. If you are also grieving, showing how you gently manage your own sadness can help model healthy coping for

them. It's okay to say, "I feel sad too, but we'll get through this together."

Let's Meet Michelle Huirama

Hi! I'm Michelle, and I write stories to help kids (and grown-ups, too) understand big feelings—especially the kind we feel when we miss someone we love.

I wrote A Hug in My Heart because I know how hard it is to say goodbye to someone as special as a Grandmother. When my own loved ones passed away, I wished for a story that could help me feel safe, understood, and not so alone. So I decided to write one.

My books are like gentle hugs made out of words. I hope this one helps you feel comforted, remember your happy memories, and know that your Grandmother's love is still with you—right there in your heart.

Thank you for reading. You're never alone on your journey.

Ko Tukotuku te Reikura

Ko Tamainupo te Hapu

Ko Karioi te Maunga

Ko Waikato te Ipukarea

Ko Tainui te Waka

With Love

Written with empathy and care,

this story reminds families that saying good-bye doesn't mean forgetting.

It means remembering with love.

And whenever you're ready, you can come back to these pages,

draw another picture, write a new memory, or just sit and remember.

Your love for your Grandmother never ends, and this book will always be here for you.

With love,

Michelle

A Healing Grief Series

for children aged 7 and up

Grief is the shape love takes when someone we care about is no longer here.
Love That Stays is a heartfelt book series designed to support older children as they navigate the complex emotions that come with loss. Whether it's a grandparent, parent, sibling, friend, or pet—these books gently walk with kids through the waves of grief, offering tools to help them remember, reflect, and begin to heal.

With compassionate language, thoughtful chapters, and creative activities like journaling, storytelling, memory-making, and mindfulness, each book invites children to explore their emotions at their own pace. These stories honor the unbreakable bond between kids and the people they love—showing that even though someone may be gone, the love they shared will always remain.

Love That Stays reminds young readers that grief is not about forgetting—it's about remembering, growing, and carrying love forward, one page at a time.

www.ingramcontent.com/pod-product-compliance
Lightning Source LLC
LaVergne TN
LVHW051225080426
835513LV00016B/1419